One Carton of Oops!

Judy Bradbury

Illustrations by Cathy Trachok

LEARNING TRIANGLE PRESS
An imprint of McGraw-Hill

New York San Francisco Washington, D.C. Auckland Bogotá Caracas
Lisbon London Madrid Mexico City Milan Montreal New Delhi
San Juan Singapore Sydney Tokyo Toronto

McGraw-Hill

A Division of The **McGraw·Hill** *Companies*

Library of Congress Cataloging-in-Publication Data

CIP

Copyright © 1997 by The McGraw-Hill Companies, Inc.
Published by Learning Triangle Press, an imprint of McGraw-Hill.

1 2 3 4 5 6 7 8 9 KPT/KPT 9 0 1 0 9 8 7 6

ISBN 0-07-007039-3

McGraw-Hill books are available at special quantity discounts to use as premiums and sales promotions, or for use in corporate training programs. For more information, please write to the Director of Special Sales, McGraw-Hill, 11 West 19th Street, New York, NY 10011. Or contact your local bookstore.

Acquisitions editor: Judith Terrill-Breuer
Teacher review: Sharon Hixon
Production team: DTP computer artist supervisor: Tess Raynor
                 DTP computer artist: Charles Burkhour
Designer: Jaclyn J. Boone   LAND1

For Gene, for ever: for believing in me,
encouraging me, loving me.
And for the title.

When his mother asked him to go to the corner
store to buy a dozen eggs, Christopher hid.

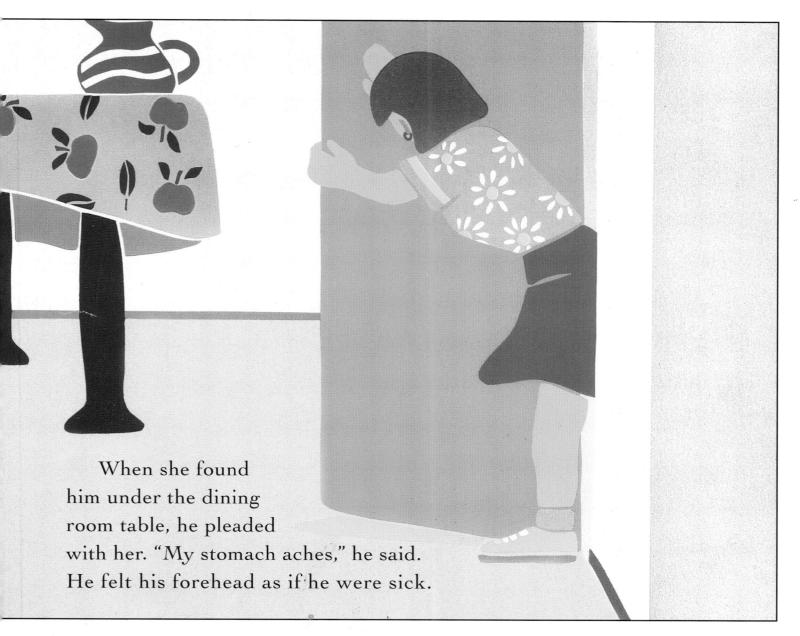

When she found
him under the dining
room table, he pleaded
with her. "My stomach aches," he said.
He felt his forehead as if he were sick.

Finally, he gave up and started off.

"It's just one measly carton," Christopher told himself.

But in that carton are **twelve** eggs, he thought.

"Twelve!" he groaned. "I'll never make it home with a dozen eggs!"

5

FRUIT

Once inside the store, Christopher headed for the dairy case. He picked up a carton of eggs, checked inside, and counted twelve.

6

He paid Mr. Skipworth
and stepped outside.

Just then
Doofus, a three-month
old, one-hundred-pound
Saint Bernard puppy, scrambled
around the corner from behind
the dumpster. He barreled down
the walkway and smacked head-on into Christopher. *And the eggs.*

8

Without stopping, Doofus continued leaping and bounding along the walkway. He was chasing a bumblebee, after all, and had no idea that he'd knocked Christopher down or that he'd never, ever catch that fuzzy, buzzing bee.

Christopher collected himself and the carton of eggs. He looked inside. One egg had broken. Instead of a dozen, he now had eleven whole eggs to take to his mother. He tried to scoop up the broken egg and put it back.

"Doofus needs a leash," Christopher decided.
"And a collar, obedience school, and a fenced-in yard!"

Just then Carmella Sanchez, with two permanently scratched knees, came zooming across the parking lot. She skidded over a narrow strip of rocks and weeds between the parking lot and the sidewalk before she lost her balance.

BAM! Whirling and twirling, Christopher
landed beneath the front tire of Carmella's bike.
Still spinning, the wheel sang rat-a-tat-tat as the
spokes slapped the open lid on the carton of eggs.

Muttering and sputtering, Carmella brushed herself off. Christopher looked down. Two more eggs were cracked. Three in all! That left nine whole eggs. He tried to scoop up the broken eggs and put them back.

"Carmella, you need a leash, too!" Christopher laughed.

Carmella raced off, ponytails flying.
"Sorry!" she shouted back. "I'm late!"

Christopher was in the middle of the street when he
heard the roar. A motorcycle zoomed toward the red
light and then screeched to a halt. Christopher sprinted
to the curb and leaped to the safety of the sidewalk.

But in his haste he missed
and landed on a puddly patch
of grass near a lawn sprinkler.
He skidded.
He slid.
He sat.

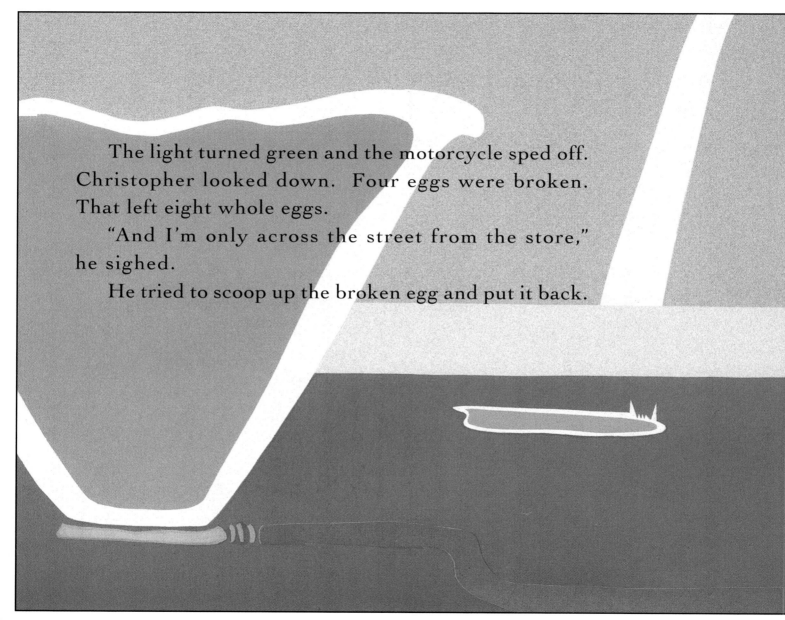

The light turned green and the motorcycle sped off.
Christopher looked down. Four eggs were broken.
That left eight whole eggs.

"And I'm only across the street from the store,"
he sighed.

He tried to scoop up the broken egg and put it back.

In the middle of the next block, Christopher passed Ms. Butcher's flower garden. Bright yellow and red blooms flashed beside soft shades of pink and peach and creamy white. There were flowers everywhere! Christopher breathed deeply, delighted by their scent. Only he must have breathed *too* deeply.

FLOWERS $1 per dozen

22

Christopher opened his eyes to find the carton of eggs lying on its side under a bush.

There were only six whole eggs left. Half of the dozen were now broken. And the carton was getting pretty messy from those six cracked and runny eggs!

25

Wiping his nose, Christopher continued down the block. His eyes itched and his nose ran, but he clutched that carton of eggs with both hands. After all, he still had six whole eggs!

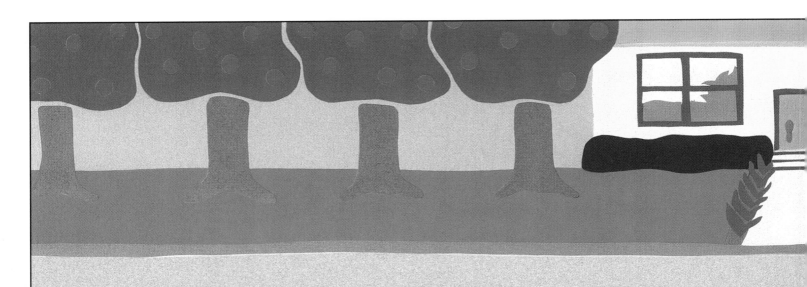

But when he thought about giving the carton of eggs to his mother, he slowed down. Six whole eggs, yes, but also six messy, runny, cracked, and broken eggs. And all twelve eggs in a soppy, sloppy, grubby cardboard carton.

Just then Christopher's sixteen-year-old
brother Anthony drove down the street.

"Stop!" Christopher yelled. He hurried to the car
and got in, placing the carton of eggs carefully
on his lap.

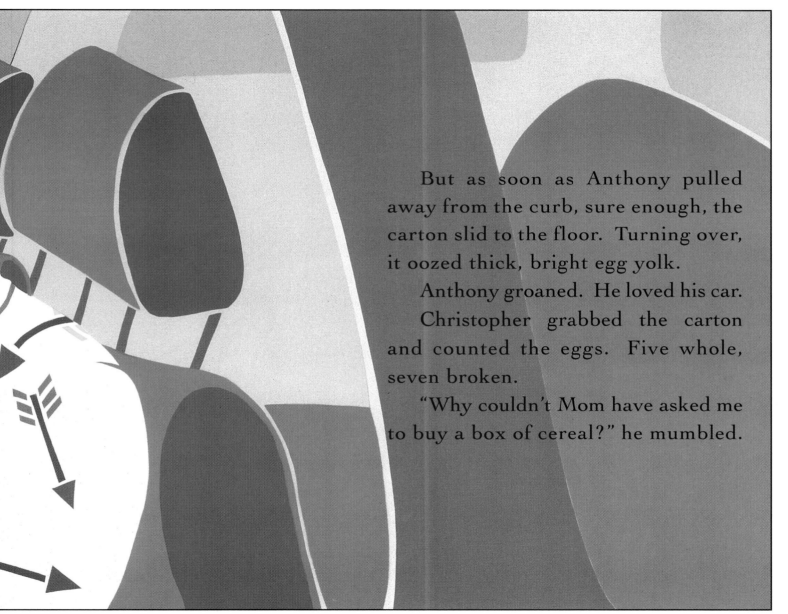

But as soon as Anthony pulled away from the curb, sure enough, the carton slid to the floor. Turning over, it oozed thick, bright egg yolk.

Anthony groaned. He loved his car.

Christopher grabbed the carton and counted the eggs. Five whole, seven broken.

"Why couldn't Mom have asked me to buy a box of cereal?" he mumbled.

Finally, they were home! Christopher had just
climbed out of the car when his little brother,
Jeffrey, spotted him. He toddled over,
shrieking with glee, as if Christopher
had just returned from a long
vacation instead of a short
trip to the corner store.

He hugged Christopher so hard
that Christopher lost his balance.

The next thing Christopher knew, he was on the ground again, Jeffrey had egg in his hair, and there were eight broken eggs. That left only four whole eggs to give to his mother. Slowly, Christopher went into the house.

At that moment Christopher
was certain he'd never enjoy a plate
of scrambled eggs again, even if he
lived to be one hundred and ten.

Christopher's mother knelt before him.
"I only need two eggs, you know," she said.

Then she gave Christopher a hug. "I'm making chocolate chip brownies for the animal shelter bake sale, and the recipe calls for just two eggs," she explained.

A smile eased its way onto Christopher's face.
Just two! And there were *four whole eggs* in the carton.
That meant there were two eggs to spare! Why,
he could even have scrambled eggs for lunch!

SUGAR
S

43

Christopher ran off
to find his brothers.

He felt certain he could interest
them in scrambled eggs and toast.

THE END

Discoveries
You can read this story, and you can count it, too!

See how many things you can count on each and every page!

- Whenever you add the number of broken eggs and unbroken eggs Christopher has, what number do you get?

How many apples are on pages 2-3?

- How many other things can you count on these pages?

Count the flowers on pages 4-5.

- How many flowers are on each side of the walkway?
- How many apples are on each tree?
- How many apples are there altogether?
- What else can you count on these pages?

Count the fruits and vegetables on pages 6-7.

- How many of each kind are there?

Count the trees behind Carmella on pages 12-13.

- Can you find something else in the picture that adds up to the same number?

How many flowers are in the garden on page 22?

- How many flowers are there of each color? You know that there are twelve items in one dozen. Do you see half of Ms. Butcher's flower sign? How much do twelve of Ms. Butcher's flowers cost?

How many unbroken eggs does Christopher have to give his mother on pages 38-39?

- Can you find that number someplace else on these pages?

There are many different shapes in this book.

- How many triangles can you find? How many circles? How many rectangles?
- Who is wearing stars?